NATURE SPOTTERS

WHAT CAN YOU SPOT IN THE MEADOWS?

What wonderful wildlife will you discover living in the meadows? See which of the 175 species featured in this book you can spot, and tick them off. When you have found 50 or more, you will have earned your top Nature Spotters certificate! Simply fill it in, tear it out from the back of the book and pin it up on your wall.

The book is divided into themes such as flowers, birds and mammals. Test your nature knowledge with the quiz questions at the start of every section, and then turn to page 76 to see how many you have answered correctly.

WILD FLOWERS

The best time to look for wild flowers is in spring and summer, when plants are busy producing seed to grow into new plants the following year. In order to produce seeds, dust-like pollen has to be transferred from the male part of a flower to the female part.

Pollen is moved by insects when they move between flowers to feed. Do you know the names of these pollinators?

COMMON POPPY

The large, crinkly petals of the poppy unfold, shine and die all within the course of one day. You are most likely to see these red flowers in cornfields and on farmland where the ground has been disturbed.

DID YOU KNOW?
Butterflies do not visit poppies because they do not produce the sugary nectar on which butterflies feed.

FOUND IN:	Cornfields, waste ground
FLOWERS:	June to August
PETALS:	4
FEATURES:	Large single flowers on thin stems
ATTRACTS:	Bees and hoverflies
HEIGHT:	Up to 60 cm

HAREBELL

By midsummer, when many other flowers are fading, harebells begin to appear in meadows and along roadsides. Most of them are this beautiful purple colour, and you may find white and pink ones, too.

FOUND IN:	Dry, grassy meadows and banks
FLOWERS:	July to September
PETALS:	5 fused petals
FEATURES:	Delicate flowers on thin stems
ATTRACTS:	Many different insects
HEIGHT:	Up to 50 cm

DID YOU KNOW?
The harebell's scientific name Campanula rotundifolia *means "little bell with rounded leaves" in Latin.*

DEVIL'S-BIT SCABIOUS

This round mass of tiny flowers has both the male parts (the anthers) and the female parts (the stigmas) sticking out. Insects brush against these as they feed, helping to pollinate the flowers.

DID YOU KNOW?
The only place where the marsh fritillary butterfly lays her eggs is on the lushest leaves of devil's-bit scabious.

FOUND IN:	Upland and marshy meadows
FLOWERS:	July to October
PETALS:	4
FEATURES:	Round flowerheads on thin stems
ATTRACTS:	Bees, moths, butterflies
HEIGHT:	Up to 70 cm

OTHER PURPLE FLOWERS

RED CLOVER
This clover is very common and flowers from May to October. In the past, pink flowers were often called "red" as there was no word for the colour pink.

SHEEP'S SORREL
Tiny bronze-red flowers hug the stems of sheep's sorrel, a plant that thrives in dry meadows. The pointed leaves may be eaten in salads when young and tender.

GREAT BURNET
This tall plant has oval, slightly waxy-looking crimson flowers. It grows in damp meadows near rivers, and flowers from June through to September.

MARSH THISTLE
In the autumn, marsh thistles produce seeds with plumes of soft, white hairs known as thistledown, on which birds feed. This plant is tall and has very sharp spikes.

COMMON KNAPWEED
This plant looks like a thistle and belongs to the same daisy family, but its stiff stems have no prickles. It flowers throughout the summer and attracts many insects.

BETONY
From early to late summer, the slightly ragged-looking flowers of betony peep up from dry grasslands. It has long been used to cure many illnesses.

TUFTED VETCH
This is a member of the pea family. Its stems wind through grassy areas, with up to 40 flowers hanging from each one. The leaves have many leaflets.

MEADOW CRANE'S-BILL
The five rounded petals of meadow crane's-bill curve slightly inwards in the shape of a bowl. It flowers all summer, and in the autumn its leaves turn red.

Speedwell

There are several types of speedwell. This is germander speedwell and it grows in almost any grassy place. At night and when the weather is bad, the flowers close to protect the pollen and nectar inside.

FOUND IN:	Fields, verges, lawns, hedges
FLOWERS:	March to July
PETALS:	4
FEATURES:	Creeping plant with flower clusters
ATTRACTS:	Butterflies & hoverflies especially
HEIGHT:	Up to 20 cm

DID YOU KNOW?
The red stems you can see above have two lines of hairs running down them – a sign that it is germander speedwell.

OTHER BLUE FLOWERS

BUGLE
You are as likely to see this spring-flowering plant in woods as in damp meadows. Most flowers are blue, but you may find white and pink ones as well.

SELF-HEAL
As its name suggests, this plant is medicinal: it contains chemicals that help reduce swellings and dry wounds. It flowers over the summer in meadows and woods.

TEASEL
Teasel flowers open in bands in July and August, starting from the centre of each prickly head. The flowers then fade and seeds form, providing food for birds.

CORNFLOWER
Like all members of the daisy family, this species has flowerheads that are each a mass of florets. The outer ones are trumpet-shaped to attract insects.

COMMON SPOTTED ORCHID

From early summer, spikes of lightly scented flowers rise up from the grass. The flowers range from pink or purple to almost white, and the long, strap-like leaves have short and long purple spots on them.

FOUND IN:	Meadows, woods, verges
FLOWERS:	June to August
PETALS:	6 (5 small petals and 1 large lip)
FEATURES:	Single stalks with flower spikes
ATTRACTS:	Mainly bees and flies
HEIGHT:	Up to 70 cm

DID YOU KNOW?
Other UK orchids have spots on their leaves, but those of the common spotted orchid are shaped like long dashes.

OTHER PINK FLOWERS

PYRAMIDAL ORCHID
From June to August, these pink pyramids grow on chalky grasslands. The flowers and leaves are plain, unlike those of the common spotted orchid.

CREEPING THISTLE
This is our most common thistle and grows to form dense patches. It flowers from June to October and produces thousands of downy seeds, on which birds feed.

CUCKOOFLOWER
The sound of the first cuckoo in spring marks the time when this delicate pink flower appears. It is a member of the cabbage family and grows in damp meadows.

RAGGED-ROBIN
This tall, pink wild flower thrives in damp meadows. The petals look as though they have been cut to ribbons, hence the name, and they have no scent.

MEADOW BUTTERCUP

With its branching stems and shiny yellow flowers, this is the tallest species of buttercup. If you look carefully, you can see a hard green knot at the centre of each flower, which is where the seeds form.

FOUND IN:	Fields, verges, hedgerows
FLOWERS:	April to August
PETALS:	5
FEATURES:	Tall with branched stems
ATTRACTS:	Insects of all kinds
HEIGHT:	Up to 1 m

DID YOU KNOW?
Try putting a buttercup flower under your chin. Folklore has it that if your skin glows yellow, it means you like butter!

COMMON RAGWORT

It is easy to spot the bright flowers of common ragwort in summer and early autumn. These flowers produce very large quantities of nectar, attracting many pollinators that need to feed before winter.

DID YOU KNOW?
This is a key plant for insects. Over 100 species feed on its large nectar stores, and others devour its jagged leaves.

FOUND IN:	Rough grassy meadows
FLOWERS:	June to October
PETALS:	10 to 16 ray florets
FEATURES:	Branched stems, flower clusters
ATTRACTS:	Insects of all kinds
HEIGHT:	Up to 1.5 m

OTHER YELLOW FLOWERS

COWSLIP
Bunches of cup-shaped flowers hang down to one side of each cowslip stem. They sway in the breeze on sunny banks and meadows from April to May.

YELLOW-RATTLE
Parasitic plants such as these suck up nutrients through their roots from nearby grasses. This weakens them and allows space for other wild flowers to flourish.

LESSER TREFOIL
The leaves of this tiny yellow flower have three leaflets like a clover. It should be easy to find in most reasonably dry meadows, especially ones that are mown.

TORMENTIL
If you see a flower like this, check the number of petals, for there are many similar plants. This one has four notched petals, and flowers from May to September.

SILVERWEED
Unlike tormentil, which looks very similar, silverweed has five yellow petals and long divided leaves with a silvery sheen. It flowers between June and August.

GOAT'S-BEARD
Interestingly, this flower opens only in the morning. It looks like a dandelion but has long green sepals around its flowers and much larger seed-heads.

HAWKWEED
This is common hawkweed, one of many hawkweed species. They can be hard to tell apart, so give yourself a tick if you spot any tall flower that looks like this.

LADY'S BEDSTRAW
Armfuls of these sweet-smelling flowers were once gathered from summer meadows and used to stuff mattresses. It is pollinated by insects such as flies and beetles.

WHITE FLOWERS

WILD CARROT
Members of the carrot family are also called umbellifers. Umbels are the flower clusters that form from stalks which look like the spokes of an umbrella.

PIGNUT
This is a strange name for a flower. It comes from the nut-brown tubers in the ground from which the plant grows. Pigs will sniff them out and eat them.

YARROW
The flowers may be white, cream or pink and are easy to spot on dry grassland from June onwards. Beetles and flies find it hard to resist a smelly plant like this.

LESSER STITCHWORT
Small, star-shaped flowers like these may be seen in dry meadows between May and August. The similar greater stitchwort grows in woodlands.

MEADOWSWEET
Wherever meadowsweet grows, there must be water nearby. In summer, its stiff, red stems are topped with canopies of strongly scented, creamy-white flowers.

WHITE CLOVER
Each one of these round flowerheads is a mass of tiny florets. These are rich in nectar and pollen and are a honeypot for all kinds of insects.

COMMON CHICKWEED
This is another plant with small, star-shaped white flowers. Unlike lesser stitchwort it has round not narrow leaves. One plant can produce 2,000 seeds in a season.

RIBWORT PLANTAIN
Clumps of ribwort plantain with long pointed leaves can be seen almost anywhere. Each flowerhead has a long stem and a ring of white stamens.

BEE ORCHID

The lower lip of the bee orchid is a velvety maroon. Both its amazing pattern and the chemicals the plant releases mimic a female bee in order to attract male bees to pollinate it. It is a thrilling plant to find.

FOUND IN:	Chalky grasslands
FLOWERS:	June to July
PETALS:	3 pink petals & 1 brown lip
FEATURES:	Tall stems with several flower buds
ATTRACTS:	Insects, especially bees
HEIGHT:	Up to 45 cm

DID YOU KNOW?
Orchids make up the largest family of flowering plants. There are about 28,000 species worldwide.

Oxeye Daisy

Like other types of daisy, this species has two types of floret making up each flowerhead – in this case, white ray florets to attract insects and yellow disc florets containing the male and female flower parts.

DID YOU KNOW?
It may surprise you to know that the daisy family, to which this belongs, includes dandelions and thistles.

FOUND IN:	All types of meadow
FLOWERS:	June to August
PETALS:	15 to 40 white ray florets
FEATURES:	Large round flowers on thin stems
ATTRACTS:	Important for all insects
HEIGHT:	Up to 60 cm

GRASSES

Every meadow has its own mix of grasses and the ones that follow are just a few of the thousands of species that exist. Of all plants, they are the most useful as food to humans.

Farmers grow particular grasses known as cereal crops. These are sown in cultivated fields and harvested each summer. Do you know which of the pictures below are the crops barley, wheat, oats and corn?

YORKSHIRE-FOG

This wonderful purple-tinged grass can be seen in almost any summer meadow. Try running your hand through it. It feels incredibly soft because all parts of the plant are covered with downy hairs.

DID YOU KNOW?
The tiny caterpillars of the small skipper butterfly hibernate inside the curled up leaves of Yorkshire-fog.

FOUND IN:	All grasslands
FLOWERS:	May to August
LEAVES:	Flat, grey-green and soft
ORIGIN:	Britain and continental Europe
FOOD FOR:	Caterpillars and rabbits
HEIGHT:	Up to 1 metre

QUAKING-GRASS

The delicate flowerheads of this grass hang down from their stems and move or quake in the slightest breeze. The flowers are purple at first, then turn to green and finally become straw-coloured.

FOUND IN:	Sunny meadows
FLOWERS:	June to August
LEAVES:	Blue-green, forming tufts
ORIGIN:	Britain and Europe
FOOD FOR:	Many farmland birds
HEIGHT:	Up to 40 cm

DID YOU KNOW?
People would leave quaking-grass out in their houses as a way to deter mice, especially if they didn't like cats.

OTHER GRASSES

MEADOW FOXTAIL
These long brown flowerheads look like fox tails, hence the name. This grass flowers from April to June and is food for livestock and some caterpillars.

TIMOTHY
This grass is easy to confuse with meadow foxtail, but the flowerheads are chunkier at the top and bottom. It is used to feed pet rabbits and guinea pigs.

COCK'S-FOOT
Farmers use cock's-foot as hay for cattle, for it grows quickly and withstands tough conditions. Unlike soft timothy, the leaves are rough with sharp edges.

SWEET VERNAL GRASS
This early-flowering grass smells sweetly of vanilla – but it can cause hayfever. Its long, thin flower spikes are easy to spot growing in meadows.

FUNGI

Fungi are not plants or animals but they are alive. They consist of millions of tiny threads, which weave through soil or decaying wood. What you see is the fruiting part known as a toadstool, often consisting of a cap and a stem.

Fungi have many different shapes and textures. Three of the organisms shown below are not a form of fungus; can you guess which ones they are?

Scots pine

Small scabious

Pink ballerina waxcap

Yellow fieldcap

Broomrape

Shaggy inkcap

FAIRY RING MUSHROOM

These small fungi are a common sight in meadows. Underground, their tiny threads take sugars from the grass around them and feed them nutrients in return, making the grass longer and greener.

DID YOU KNOW?
If this fungus dries out completely, it does not die. All it needs is to absorb some water for it to spring back to life.

FOUND IN:	Short grass
FRUITS:	April to November
COLOUR:	Beige cap; whitish stem
FEATURES:	Large numbers grow together
WARNING:	Similar to deadly fool's funnel
SIZE:	8 cm

GIANT PUFFBALL

Fungi produce tiny cells called spores to create new fungi. The giant puffball is one of the largest fungi in the world and produces trillions of these spores, which are released as the puffball ages or is damaged.

FOUND IN:	Grasslands, often near nettles
FRUITS:	July to September
COLOUR:	White at first, becoming yellowish
FEATURES:	Can be as large as a football!
WARNING:	Do not breath in the spores
SIZE:	Up to 80 cm

DID YOU KNOW?
There is no other living organism on Earth that produces as many spores or seeds as the giant puffball.

OTHER FUNGI

SCARLET WAXCAP
Waxcaps appear in meadows in late summer and autumn. This is just one of many waxcap species, which grow in ancient grasslands with poor, infertile soils.

PARASOL MUSHROOM
Rising up out of the grass, these elegant, long-stemmed mushrooms are easy to spot. The caps open with age and are covered with brown scales.

YELLOW CLUB
These thin fungi grow to about 7 cm from grassy or mossy sites. They look like yellow tentacles and have no cap or gills, unlike the other mushrooms here.

FIELD MUSHROOM
This is one of the best-known fungi and is found in grassy areas from summer to autumn. The gills are pink at first and turn brown gradually.

INSECTS

In spring, summer and autumn, meadows are alive with insects of every kind. Colourful butterflies flitting between flowers are easy to spot, but many other insects are much harder to find, especially if they are green! Below you can find a butterfly, a beetle, a dragonfly, a hoverfly and a moth. All of these species live in meadow habitats. Do you know which type of insect each of them is?

Cinnabar

Hornet mimic

Ruddy darter

Essex skipper

Rose chafer

COMMON BLUE

If you see a flash of blue darting between low-growing wild flowers in the summer, it could well be a male common blue. This is the male with its bright blue wings; the female has brown upperwings.

DID YOU KNOW? *Butterflies roost at night and in wet weather. Common blues roost head down on grasses, sometimes in groups.*	
FOUND IN:	Flower-rich meadows & grasslands
FLIES:	May to June; July to October
FEEDS ON:	Adults sip nectar from flowers
LARVAE:	Caterpillars feed on trefoil
ADULTS:	Females are mostly brown
WINGSPAN:	Up to 38 mm

MARBLED WHITE

The bold markings are a sign to predators that this butterfly is poisonous. Like all butterflies, it needs to warm up in the sun before it can fly. It then spends much of the day nectaring on purple flowers.

FOUND IN:	Flowery grasslands
SEEN:	June to August
FEEDS ON:	Adults sip nectar from flowers
LARVAE:	Caterpillars feed on grasses
ADULTS:	Male and female look alike
WINGSPAN:	Up to 58 mm

DID YOU KNOW?
The big surprise about the marbled white is that despite its colouring it is a member of the brown butterfly family.

MEADOW BROWN

This is one of our commonest butterflies, found in almost any grassy area, flying in all but the heat of the day. Its long feeding tube, called a proboscis, dips into each flower searching for sugary nectar.

DID YOU KNOW?	
If this butterfly is threatened by a bird, it flashes the spots on its upperwings to look like a much larger animal.	

FOUND IN:	Many types of grassland
SEEN:	May to September
FEEDS ON:	Adults sip nectar from flowers
LARVAE:	Caterpillars feed on grasses
ADULTS:	Female has orange areas on wings
WINGSPAN:	Up to 60 mm

PAINTED LADY

This incredible insect is one of the world's long-distance travellers: it migrates from Africa each spring. Some years there may be millions of painted ladies in the UK; in others there may be a few hundred.

FOUND IN:	Dry grasslands
SEEN:	May to June; July to October
FEEDS ON:	Adults sip nectar from flowers
LARVAE:	Caterpillars feed on thistles
ADULTS:	Male and female look alike
WINGSPAN:	Up to 74 mm

DID YOU KNOW?
The painted lady is the most widespread butterfly in the world and is found on almost every continent.

OTHER BUTTERFLIES

LARGE SKIPPER
This butterfly is not exactly large: it is about the size of a grape. You may catch sight of it flitting between meadow flowers between June and August.

GREEN-VEINED WHITE
Damp meadows are home to the green-veined white. It flies from April to June and from July to October, feeding on flowers such as buttercups, bugle and mint.

DARK GREEN FRITILLARY
Although this butterfly is mostly orange, there is a green sheen on its lower hindwings. It flies from July to August and takes nectar from purple wild flowers.

RINGLET
No other butterfly has markings like the ringlet's, although the number of gold circles may vary. It flies in light rain when most other butterflies are roosting.

Six-Spot Burnet

Most moths fly at night but there are some, such as this one, that are day-flying. There are several species of burnet moth, which look very similar, but this is the only one to have six spots.

FOUND IN:	Flowery grasslands
SEEN:	June to August
FEEDS ON:	Adults sip nectar from flowers
LARVAE:	Caterpillars feed on trefoil
ADULTS:	Male and female look alike
WINGSPAN:	Up to 40 mm

DID YOU KNOW?
The red colour warns predators that it is poisonous, for this moth converts the food it eats as a caterpillar into acid.

Mother Shipton

Mother Shipton was a 16th-century witch, and a hag-like face may be seen in the pattern on the upperwings of this grassland moth. It is another day-flying moth – one that is active only in sunshine.

DID YOU KNOW?
Many caterpillars feed during the day, but those of this moth feed at night. It is a good way to avoid being seen.

FOUND IN:	A range of grasslands
SEEN:	May to July
FEEDS ON:	Adults feed on clovers, buttercups
LARVAE:	Caterpillars feed on clovers, grasses
ADULTS:	Male and female look alike
WINGSPAN:	Up to 30 mm

GREEN BOTTLE FLY

A female green bottle fly lays around 200 eggs at a time and may lay up to 3,000 eggs in her short lifetime. The flies feed on damp, decaying matter and are a common sight around farmland.

FOUND IN:	Anywhere, especially near farms
SEEN:	Spring to autumn
FEEDS ON:	A range of living & dead matter
LARVAE:	Maggots feed on dead animals
ADULTS:	Male and female look alike
LENGTH:	Up to 14 mm

DID YOU KNOW?
In certain cases, green bottle larvae, known as maggots, are placed on patients' wounds to help them heal.

OTHER FLIES

HORSE-FLY
Most of the time, horse-flies feed on nectar and are important pollinators. But beware the female horse-fly: she bites as she needs blood to produce eggs!

DUNG FLY
This is a yellow dung fly. These flies are very important meadow creatures. Their maggots break down animal droppings so they can be absorbed into the soil.

HOVERFLY
Try watching a hoverfly. It moves like a helicopter in any direction and can hover, unlike most other insects. There are well over 250 species of hoverfly in the UK.

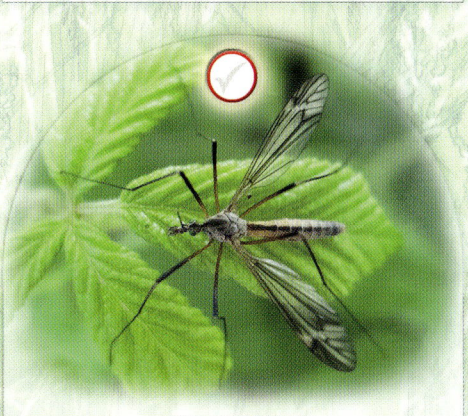

CRANEFLY
Often called a daddy long-legs, this is our largest fly. It is most active at night and you are likely to see it in meadows in late summer and autumn.

FROGHOPPER

In spring, bubbles known as "cuckoo spit" appear on plants. They are made by the young nymph of the froghopper insect. It squirts bubbles out of its rear end, then lives within the bubbles for protection.

FOUND ON:	Stems of grasses and wildflowers
SEEN:	Spring
FEEDS ON:	Plant sap (a sugary liquid)
YOUNG:	100 to 200 eggs
ADULTS:	Small, pale brown or green insects
LENGTH:	Up to 5 mm

DID YOU KNOW?
"Cuckoo spit" gets its name because it is first seen about the time cuckoos return from Africa and start calling.

YELLOW MEADOW ANT

Some old meadows look lumpy, with many little grassy mounds. These are formed by yellow meadow ants, which spend most of their lives hidden inside the hillocks or in tunnels further below ground.

DID YOU KNOW?
These ants sip sugary honeydew – a substance produced by insects called aphids, which live inside the ant nests.

FOUND IN:	Old meadows, lawns, rough grass
SEEN:	All year
FEEDS ON:	Other insects and sweet honeydew
YOUNG:	Queen ants lay thousands of eggs
ADULTS:	Yellow or brown ants
LENGTH:	Up to 4 mm

COMMON CARDER BEE

Every meadow is likely to have some of these small bumblebees buzzing around. The worker bees gather pollen from flowers, which they store on their back legs, ready to take back to their nest.

FOUND ON:	Many meadow flowers
SEEN:	Spring to autumn
FEEDS ON:	Nectar and pollen
YOUNG:	Nests house a few hundred eggs
ADULTS:	Ginger body; dark stripes on tail
LENGTH:	Around 1.5 cm

DID YOU KNOW?
Thick body hair allows bumblebees to stay active in cool conditions such as early in the morning and late in the year.

OTHER BEES

WHITE-TAILED BUMBLEBEE
This large bumblebee with its pure white tail often visits clover, thistles and knapweed. Buff-tailed bumblebees look similar but have darker, creamy-white tails.

RED-TAILED BUMBLEBEE
The bottom third of this bee is orangey red, making it easy to identify. Like other bumblebees, it lives in small colonies containing up to 200 worker bees.

CHOCOLATE MINING BEE
Meadows are home to many kinds of mining bee. They dig out nesting chambers in patches of bare earth in the ground for their eggs and larvae.

HONEYBEE
Meadow flowers are vitally important sources of nectar and pollen for honeybees. They use the nectar to make honey and feed the pollen to their young.

BEETLE GALLERY

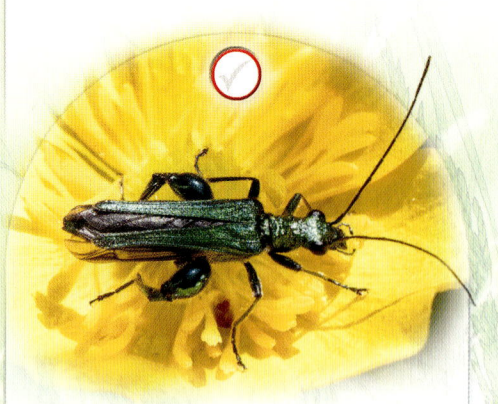

THICK-LEGGED FLOWER BEETLE
The males of this shiny beetle have swollen thighs on their back legs. The species feeds on and helps pollinate many flowers.

DOR BEETLE
The dor beetle lives in meadows where animals graze. The beetle uses its legs to bury chunks of dung on which the young beetle grubs, or larvae, feed.

BLOODY-NOSED BEETLE
If this beetle feels threatened, it squirts a foul-tasting red liquid – not real blood – out of its mouth to put off predators. The beetle feeds on the leaves of flowers.

GLOWWORM
On warm summer evenings, a light sometimes flashes on and off in meadows. It is a chemical reaction in the tail of a female glowworm, to attract males.

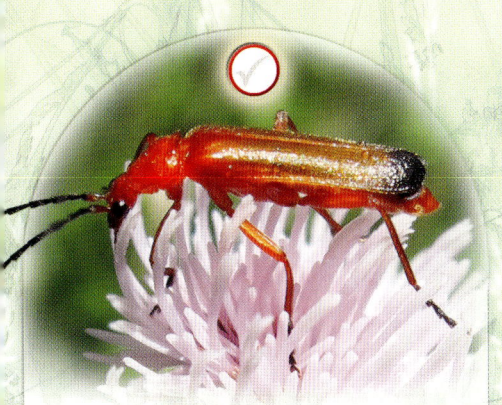

RED SOLDIER BEETLE
When the sun comes out, these beetles are seen crawling over the top of meadow flowers. The male and female spend a long time together while they mate.

GROUND BEETLE
Ground beetles move fast to hunt insects, slugs, worms and other invertebrates. Many species are black with a purple, green or gold sheen to them.

COCKCHAFER
This large beetle spends most of its life as a grub underground, where it munches the roots of meadow plants. The adult beetle comes out at night in spring.

DOCK BEETLE
The leaves of dock plants are the favourite food of this small beetle. Although it is bright and shiny and has a golden sheen, it can be quite hard to see on green leaves.

MEADOW GRASSHOPPER

Male grasshoppers chirp a "song" to attract a partner among the grass stalks, by rubbing one leg against the front of a wing. The meadow grasshopper's song is a fast buzz lasting up to five seconds.

FOUND IN:	Meadows, rough grasslands, verges
SEEN:	Summer
FEEDS ON:	Grasses
YOUNG:	Like mini versions of the adults
ADULTS:	Green, with short antennae
LENGTH:	Up to 2 cm

DID YOU KNOW?
Grasshoppers leap powerfully and can also fly. Their ears are on the sides of their bodies, tucked under the wings.

OTHER GRASSHOPPERS

COMMON GREEN GRASSHOPPER
Damp meadows suit this little grasshopper best. It is the loudest grasshopper in Britain, with a song that sounds like fast clicking.

COMMON FIELD GRASSHOPPER
Living in short grass, this grasshopper has a song that lasts for under a second and sounds like someone scraping wood.

SPECKLED BUSH-CRICKET
Bush-crickets may remind you of grasshoppers, but they have even longer back legs and enormous antennae. This one perches in hedges or bushes.

ROESEL'S BUSH-CRICKET
The song of this brown bush-cricket is like the crackle made by electricity cables overhead. Warmer summers are helping this cricket to spread northwards.

OTHER INVERTEBRATES

Invertebrates – which include insects – all lack a spine, or backbone. In fact, they do not have a single bone in their bodies! Among the tangled plant stalks and in the soil below, meadows are home to a host of other spineless creatures in addition to insects, including woodlice, slugs and worms.

Can you tell which of these meadow species have backbones (vertebrates) and which ones do not (invertebrates)?

Grass snake

Wolf spider

Marsh frog

Ladybird

Fox

Glass snail

HARVESTMAN

Harvestmen look like spiders but do not have venom and cannot spin webs. Their eight legs are long and spindly, so their pea-shaped bodies look small by comparison. They scavenge plants and dead animals.

DID YOU KNOW?
Harvestmen are so-called as they appear late in the year when farmers are bringing in the harvest.

FOUND ON:	Any meadow vegetation
SEEN:	End of summer and autumn
FEEDS ON:	Almost anything
YOUNG:	Female lays up to 100 or so eggs
ADULTS:	Like a spindly brown spider
LEGSPAN:	Up to 3 cm

CRAB SPIDER

Perched perfectly still among the petals, a crab spider waits for an insect to land on a flower, then grabs it in its long front legs. Some species can change their colour to match their flowery background.

FOUND ON:	Meadow flowers
SEEN:	Summer
FEEDS ON:	Bees, butterflies and other insects
YOUNG:	Female lays several dozen eggs
ADULTS:	Female bigger than male
LEGSPAN:	Up to 1 cm

DID YOU KNOW?
Just like a crab at the seashore, this spider holds its legs out at the side of its body and can move sideways!

OTHER SPIDERS

WASP SPIDER
One of the largest spiders in Britain, the wasp spider is a new arrival from Europe. The huge stripy female spins a big web high up among plant stems.

MONEY SPIDER
Money spiders are often ant-sized, but despite being small, they spin beautiful webs like lacy hammocks. The silky structures are commonly seen in autumn.

NURSERY WEB SPIDER
These spiders race over the ground to catch prey, and while they do not make webs, the female spins a silky, tent-like nursery for her babies.

FOUR-SPOT ORB-WEAVER
Look carefully and you will see four pale spots on this plump body. Many orb-weavers are yellowish green, but some can be brown or orange, with stripy legs.

BROWN-LIPPED SNAIL

Snails stay in damp parts of the meadow and usually emerge only after sunset. They feed by scraping plants with their rasping tongues, called radulas. Buttercups and stinging nettles are favourite foods.

FOUND ON:	Grasses and wild flowers
SEEN:	Spring to autumn
FEEDS ON:	Leaves and stems
YOUNG:	Lays up to 100 eggs at a time
ADULTS:	Brown shell with dark bands
LENGTH:	Shell is up to 2.5 cm

DID YOU KNOW?
Snail shells are made of calcium carbonate, and female birds feed on them to help form the shells of their eggs.

EARTHWORM

A meadow can have two million earthworms in an area the size of a football pitch, and every year they churn soil weighing as much as five cars. They come to the surface at night or after rain.

DID YOU KNOW?
Earthworms have no eyes or ears, and find food using thousands of tiny taste buds all over their long, slimy bodies.

FOUND IN:	Meadow soil
SEEN:	All year
FEEDS ON:	Dead plant matter
YOUNG:	Produces several hundred eggs
ADULTS:	Purplish red
LENGTH:	Up to 15 cm

Mammals

Meadows shelter lots of small mammals, including voles, mice and shrews, which spend their lives amongst grasses and other plants. They provide food for predators such as foxes, weasels and stoats, as well as birds of prey. Deer, rabbits and hares nibble the plentiful vegetation, mostly at night.

Four out of the six animals shown below are mammals. Can you work out which ones they are?

Small copper

Badger

Bat

Bullfinch

Muntjac

Hedgehog

ROE DEER

These small deer venture out of woods to graze fields, either on their own or in small groups. Only the male deer, called bucks, have antlers. When alarmed, they bark like a dog to alert other deer to the danger.

DID YOU KNOW?
Roe-deer mothers give birth in May and June. Their young, known as kids, have spotty coats and hide in long grass.

FOUND IN:	Field edges
SEEN:	All year
FEEDS ON:	Grasses and leaves
YOUNG:	2 or 3 kids
ADULTS:	Small deer with white bottom
LENGTH:	60 to 75 cm at the shoulder

RABBIT

Families of rabbits dig their networks of burrows, called warrens, in places with loose soil, often on sloping ground near hedges or trees. When grazing they stay nearby, ready to dash underground.

FOUND IN:	Field edges
SEEN:	Mainly spring to autumn
FEEDS ON:	Grasses and leaves
YOUNG:	Up to 7 kits per litter
ADULTS:	Male bigger than female
LENGTH:	Up to 40 cm

DID YOU KNOW?
Our wild rabbits originally came from Spain, and were probably brought to Britain by the Romans.

BROWN HARE

Hares are built for speed, with much longer legs than rabbits, and also have longer ears, with black tips. Unlike rabbits, they do not dig burrows, but stay above ground all year round.

DID YOU KNOW?
Hares can sprint at 45 mph. Mothers hide their babies and visit only once a day, at sunset, to feed them.

FOUND IN:	Large, open fields
SEEN:	All year
FEEDS ON:	Grasses and leaves
YOUNG:	2 to 4 leverets per litter
ADULTS:	Like large, long-legged rabbits
LENGTH:	52 to 60 cm

STOAT

Elegant and long-bodied, the stoat preys mainly on rabbits, catching them with a burst of speed. It belongs to the mustelid family, which also includes the weasel. Its tail has a telltale black tip.

FOUND IN:	Field edges
SEEN:	All year
FEEDS ON:	Small mammals, birds and eggs
YOUNG:	6 to 12 kits
ADULTS:	Sleek body; black tip on tail
LENGTH:	24 to 30 cm (without tail)

DID YOU KNOW?
Male stoats play no part in looking after their young. In winter, some, but not all, stoats develop pure-white coats.

WEASEL

So tiny that it could squeeze through a wedding ring, the weasel is nevertheless a fierce hunter. It often chases voles and mice in their tunnels, and kills them with a quick bite to the neck.

DID YOU KNOW?
Weasels begin to hunt at just 1 or 2 months old. They often take over old burrows abandoned by other mammals.

FOUND IN:	Field edges
SEEN:	All year
FEEDS ON:	Voles and mice
YOUNG:	4 to 6 kits
ADULTS:	Tiny; all-brown tail
LENGTH:	17 to 21 cm (without tail)

Fox

Fields are an excellent habitat for foxes, with a plentiful supply of food, from rabbits and voles to young birds, beetles and earthworms. Foxes also scavenge the bodies of dead animals, particularly in winter.

FOUND:	Almost everywhere
SEEN:	All year
FEEDS ON:	A range of prey and scraps
YOUNG:	3 to 5 cubs
ADULTS:	Male is larger than female
LENGTH:	Up to 90 cm (without tail)

DID YOU KNOW?
During the breeding season (mainly January and February), foxes' barks and screams can be heard at night.

SMALL MAMMALS

FIELD VOLE
Also called the short-tailed vole, this round rodent feeds on a wide range of leaves and plant stems. In some years the population of field voles booms.

MOLE
A line of molehills tells you a mole has been tunnelling in search of worms. Mole tunnels may be hundreds of metres long and several metres deep.

COMMON SHREW
Shrews bustle through the undergrowth in search of invertebrate prey. They have an excellent sense of smell but, with tiny eyes, cannot see well.

HARVEST MOUSE
Our tiniest mammal climbs among grass stalks and tall crops, using its long, strong tail as a fifth limb. It weaves a spherical nest from dry vegetation.

BELTED GALLOWAY

This traditional breed of cattle is famous for its unusual black-and-white coat, which is also woolly, making the cow tough enough to survive cold, wet weather. It thrives on a diet of rough grass.

ORIGIN:	Galloway in southern Scotland
SEEN:	Outdoors all year
FEEDS ON:	Grass
YOUNG:	Single calf once a year
ADULTS:	White stripe around middle
WEIGHT:	Up to 900 kg (bull)/600 kg (cow)

DID YOU KNOW?
With their trampling, Belted Galloways help to open up the grass, allowing more wild flowers to grow.

EXMOOR PONY

The Exmoor is among the oldest pony breeds in Britain, with a stocky body, shaggy mane, short legs and a light-coloured muzzle. It has a wild nature and in some hilly country is allowed to roam freely.

DID YOU KNOW? *Shepherds used to ride Exmoor ponies to check their flocks of sheep. Today, only a few hundred remain.*	ORIGIN: Exmoor in south-west England SEEN: Outdoors all year FEEDS ON: Grass YOUNG: Single foal once a year ADULTS: Heavy build, rich brown coat LENGTH: Up to 1.3 m at the shoulder

TRADITIONAL SHEEP

SUFFOLK
This is one of the most familiar breeds of sheep in British meadows. It was first kept in Suffolk, south-east England, and farmers say it has a gentle nature.

TEXEL
Strong and muscular, Texels are sheep that came from the Netherlands. They are now a common breed, sometimes kept in flocks of hundreds.

HERDWICK
The Herdwick lives mainly on the hills of the Lake District in north-west England. Its coat is a blue-grey colour. Flocks move up onto higher ground in summer.

BLUE-FACED LEICESTER
Sheep belonging to this old breed have a long nose that slopes gently downwards. The coat is shaggy and curly, producing plenty of fine, soft wool.

JACOB
Jacob sheep are named after a shepherd in the Bible. His flock is thought to have looked similar, with blotchy coats in a mixture of dark and pale wool.

SHETLAND
Shetland sheep can be brown, black, grey or white, and always have thick coats. They are an ancient, tough breed, kept for the quality of their soft, fine wool.

HEBRIDEAN
This tough breed originated in the Hebrides – remote islands to the west of Scotland. The sheep have mainly black wool and usually have curled horns.

ROUGH FELL
Conditions on the hills and mountains of northern England can be harsh. Rough fell sheep have thick wool and a black nose, usually with a white patch.

Birds

Meadows come alive in spring with the song of birds such as skylarks and yellowhammers. Some nest in nearby hedges and trees, others in the grass itself. Later, in autumn and winter, flocks visit meadows to feed on wild flower seeds.

Many male birds are more colourful than their female partners. Can you match up the male birds below to their female partners on the bottom row?

House sparrow

Pheasant

Reed bunting

1

2

3

KESTREL

This handsome, long-winged falcon is a vole-hunter which hovers in mid-air when it sees a rustle below, then drops like a stone to seize its prey in its talons. If voles are scarce, it switches to hunting insects.

DID YOU KNOW?
Kestrels often raise families in nest boxes. They sometimes follow hunting barn owls and steal their catch.

SEEN:	All year
FEEDS ON:	Voles, mice and insects
NEST:	Crow/magpie nest, or hole in tree
YOUNG:	4 or 5 chicks
ADULTS:	Male has grey head and tail
WINGSPAN:	70 to 80 cm

BUZZARD

Buzzards are medium-sized predators that hunt just about anything. They soar high in the sky on their broad wings, with wingtips spread like outstretched fingers, and often fly in small family groups.

SEEN:	All year
FEEDS ON:	Animals up to rabbit size; carrion
NEST:	Large stick nest in tall tree
YOUNG:	2 to 4 chicks
ADULTS:	Female is larger than male
WINGSPAN:	Up to 1.25 m

DID YOU KNOW?
Buzzards are the commonest bird of prey in Britain. Listen for their mewing cries, especially in summer.

Red Kite

Once nearly extinct in Britain, the red kite has been reintroduced and can now be seen soaring over many of our meadows. It has a long tail with a deep "V" in it and flies with graceful wingbeats.

DID YOU KNOW? *Unusually for birds of prey, kites are sociable, so are often seen in groups. In winter, they gather in large flocks.*	
SEEN:	All year
FEEDS ON:	Insects, worms and carrion
NEST:	Large stick nest in tall tree
YOUNG:	1 to 3 chicks
ADULTS:	Male and female look alike
WINGSPAN:	1.8 to 1.9 m

Swallow

The return of swallows in April from Africa has long been a welcome sign of spring. They swoop and glide low over fields, with their bills open to scoop up flies and other insects, often twittering as they go.

SEEN:	April to September
FEEDS ON:	Flying insects
NEST:	Mud cup built in barn or shed
YOUNG:	2 broods of 4 or 5 chicks
ADULTS:	Male has longer tail streamers
WINGSPAN:	32 to 34 cm

DID YOU KNOW?
It was once thought that swallows hibernated in ponds! Their nests contain about 1,300 beakfuls of mud.

SKYLARK

As he climbs high in the sky, the male skylark sings his sweet song. On the ground, this streaky brown bird can be tricky to see as it moves among meadow vegetation.

DID YOU KNOW? *Skylarks start singing in the dark, before dawn. Usually, they sing for several minutes non-stop.*	**SEEN:** All year **FEEDS ON:** Insects in summer, seeds in winter **NEST:** Woven cup hidden on ground **YOUNG:** 3 or 4 chicks **ADULTS:** Male and female look alike **WINGSPAN:** 32 to 34 cm

LARGE BIRDS

BARN OWL
These owls can be seen hunting over meadows around dawn and dusk, and occasionally in daylight hours when there are hungry chicks to feed.

SNIPE
Snipe have one of the longest bills of any wading bird. The tip of it is flexible, helping it find food in the mud. Snipe visit damp meadows in summer to breed.

PHEASANT
These extremely common meadow birds come from Central Asia. Both sexes have long tails, but the all-brown females lack the males' colourful plumage.

WOOD PIGEON
These pigeons are often seen in fields of crops as they nibble green shoots, spilled grain and wild flower seeds. They breed almost all year round.

STOCK DOVE
Stock doves lack the white neck patch of wood pigeons and have a brighter green-and-purple sheen to the head and breast. They feed on crops and seeds.

ROOK
Rooks search for food in flocks and nest in treetop colonies called rookeries. Their long, grey beaks and bare faces help you to tell them apart from crows.

CARRION CROW
Carrion is the word for dead animals, yet despite its name, this crow also eats seeds, insects and young birds. Crows are sociable, adaptable and intelligent birds.

JACKDAW
A series of loud "chak chak" calls may alert you that this small type of crow is around. After forming a pair, the male and female stay partners for years.

BLACK-HEADED GULL

Flocks of these red-legged gulls appear on farmland in winter, and follow ploughs to snap up insects or worms disturbed as the tractors rumble past. In their winter plumage, their heads are mostly white.

SEEN:	Mainly in winter
FEEDS ON:	Insects, worms, seeds, scraps
NEST:	On the ground in marshes
YOUNG:	1 to 4 chicks
ADULTS:	Male and female look alike
WINGSPAN:	Around 1.1 m

DID YOU KNOW?
Black-headed gulls are misnamed as they have dark brown, not black, heads – and only in their summer plumage.

LAPWING

Lapwings prefer wet meadows with short grass. They have a "floppy" way of flying with paddle-shaped wings, and the male's courtship display involves much zigzagging as he tumbles through the air.

DID YOU KNOW?
The old country name for lapwing is "peewit", which is what their strangely wheezy, squeaky call sounds like.

SEEN:	All year
FEEDS ON:	Invertebrates such as worms
NEST:	Simple scrape in the earth
YOUNG:	3 or 4 chicks
ADULTS:	Male and female look alike
WINGSPAN:	82 to 85 cm

MEADOW SONGBIRDS

YELLOWHAMMER
Yellowhammers often perch on top of bushes or hedges at the edge of meadows. Here the male performs his repetitive, high-pitched song all summer long.

REED BUNTING
Reed buntings visit meadows mainly in autumn and winter, when they join flocks of other birds. Females lack the black-and-white head pattern of males.

GOLDFINCH
These pretty songbirds have tinkling, musical calls. The birds feed in flocks, using their pointed bills to take small seeds from wild flowers such as thistles.

LINNET
Male linnets have a rosy-red forehead and breast. The females are plainer, to help hide them on the nest. Linnets are seed-eaters with a twittering summer song.

HOUSE SPARROW
Flocks of sparrows nest around farms and feed in nearby fields, mostly on insects in summer and seeds at other times. Females lack the males' black throat patch.

TREE SPARROW
Tree sparrows do not spend that much time in trees! They are uncommon and look brighter than house sparrows. Most live on wildlife-friendly farms.

WHITETHROAT
Whitethroats are summer visitors to Britain which arrive in April and leave in September. They are hard to spot as they hide in brambles and thick hedges.

MEADOW PIPIT
These streaky little birds spend the summer in hills and mountains, and the winter on farmland. They creep around and make "seep seep" calls in flight.

QUIZ ANSWERS

WILD FLOWERS
The names of the pollinators are as follows:
1. Ant 2. Moth 3. Bumblebee 4. Beetle
5. Honeybee 6. Hoverfly 7. Butterfly

•

GRASSES
The names of the cereal crops are as follows:
1. Wheat 2. Barley 3. Oats 4. Corn

•

FUNGI
The three organisms that are not fungi are the Scots pine, the small scabious and the broomrape.

•

INSECTS
Cinnabar = moth • Hornet mimic = hoverfly
Ruddy darter = dragonfly • Essex skipper = butterfly
Rose chafer = beetle

•

OTHER INVERTEBRATES
The animals with backbones (known as vertebrates) are the grass snake, the marsh frog and the fox. The animals without backbones (known as invertebrates) are the wolf spider, the ladybird and the glass snail.

•

MAMMALS
The mammals are the badger, the bat, the muntjac deer and the hedgehog.

•

BIRDS
1. Pheasant 2. Reed bunting 3. House sparrow

ACKNOWLEDGEMENTS

GUEST AUTHOR: Ben Hoare
Scientific adviser: Dr Trevor Dines
Production adviser: Yolanta Motylinska
Editor: Katie Crous; Proofreader: Penny Phillips
Prepress designer: Les Hunt
Foreign rights: Odette Lusby, Boundless Books 4 All

PICTURE CREDITS
© Shutterstock

p6 Burnet: Andy Shell; p20 Oats: E.O.; p22 Quaking grass: Martin Flowler; p23 Timothy: Artturi; p24 Yellow fieldcap: Henri Koskinen; Pink ballerina waxcap: Graeme Pearce; p25 Fairy ring mushroom: Olga S photography; p27 Scarlet wax cap: Christopher Slesarchik; Yellow club fungus: Henri Koskinen; Field mushroom: Johannes Dag Mayer; p28 Cinnabar: Marek R. Swadzba; Common darter dragonfly: Stefan Rotter; p35 Mother shipton: Keith Hider; p37 Yellow dung fly: Jolanda Aalbers; p41 Mining bee: Wirestock Creators; p42 Dor beetle: Andrew Buckin; Glowworm: Igor Krasilov; p45 Common green grasshopper: Marek R. Swadzba; p46 Grass snake: Stephan Morris; Wolf spider: kurt_G; Glass snail: Vinicius R. Souza; p49 Money spider: Anton Kozyrev; Four spot orb-weaver: SchererT; p52 Bat: Rudmer Zwerver; Bullfinch: Olga Lipatova; Muntjac: Sandra Standbridge; p53 Roe deer: Soru Epotok; p55 Brown hare: WildlifeWorld; p56 Stoat: Thierry de Villeroche; p57 Weasel: Stephan Morris; p58 Fox: Vaclav Matous; p59 Field vole: Rudmer Zwerver; Common shrew: Erni; Harvest mouse: Paul Tymon; p60 Belted galloway: vagabond54; p61 Exmoor pony: Karen Brouwer; p62 Suffolk: Pyty; Texel: Anne Coatesy; Blue-faced Leicester: Ballygally View Images; p63 Shetland: Peter Turner Photography; Hebridean: Reinhold Leitner; p64 Reed bunting (M): Erni; Reed bunting (F): Veselin Gramatikov; p65 Kestrel: Clive Ferreira; p66 Buzzard: Piotr Krzeslak; p67 Red kite: Rafal Szozda; p68 Swallow: Gallinago_media; p69 Skylark: Edgar Smislov; p70 Snipe: Antonio Ramos; p71 Stock dove: Erni; Rook: Rudmer Zwerver; p72 Black-headed gull: Richard Constantinoff; p73 Lapwing: Rudmer Zwerver; p74 Yellowhammer: AlekseyKarpenko; Reed bunting: Erni; Goldfinch: KasperczakBohdan; Linnet: SanderMeertinsPhotography; p75 Tree sparrow: Johannes Dag Mayer; Meadow pipit: Andrew M. Allport

Icon images:
Flowers and grasses: iana; Fungi: Alfmaler; Insects: Z-art; Invertebrates: Yulia Bulgakova; Mammals: Natalllenka.m; Birds: elisabetaaa

p18 Bee orchid © Dr Trevor Dines

All other photos © Fine Feather Press

WARNING!
Please do not collect or eat any of the plants or fungi that you spot outside – they may be poisonous.

First published in 2023 by Fine Feather Press Limited
The Coach House, Elstead Road, Farnham, Surrey GU10 1JE
EU enquiries: Andrea Pinnington, 2022 Route de Laurélie,
12270 Bor-et-Bar, France
Copyright © 2023 Fine Feather Press Limited

All rights reserved. No part of this publication may be reproduced, stored in a retrieval system or transmitted in any form or by any means, electronic, mechanical, photocopying, recording or otherwise, without the prior permission of the publishers.

2 4 6 8 10 9 7 5 3 1

A CIP catalogue record is available from the British Library
ISBN: 978-1-908489-73-9
Printed in China

Fine Feather Press Ltd makes every effort to ensure that the papers used in its books are made from trees that have been legally sourced from well-managed and credibly certified forests.

www.finefeatherpress.com